Hard-Won Cowboy Wisdom

(Not Necessarily in Order of Importance.)

Peter Coe Verbica

Bonus: Includes the cowboy poem "I grew up"

Hard-Won Cowboy Wisdom:
(Not Necessarily in Order of Importance.)

© 2015 by Peter Coe Verbica
ISBN: 9780991153541 [print edition]

Revised edition.

ISBN: 0991153545
Library of Congress Control Number: 2015917684
Peter Coe Verbica, San Jose, CA

~ Second Printing ~

The photograph of Vanessa Verbica on a hunter jumper © C. Cammett.

The poem "I grew up" © 2012 by Peter Coe Verbica. All rights reserved. Excerpt from "The Ascension," © 2001 and 2013 by Peter Coe Verbica. All rights reserved.

Ranch rodeo photograph on the book's cover is from *Rancho San Felipe* (the Coe Ranch in Santa Clara County, Calif.) and features Britt Gruwell riding a wild horse, with his brother watching; Sheriff Landford judges the merits of the horsemanship and awards the prizes. (Circa 1899.)

(Photograph from the author's collection.)

Published by Peter Coe Verbica
San Jose, California

Coe Brothers' hunting cabin at Coe Flat (Pine Ridge,
now a part of Henry Coe State Park, Morgan Hill, Calif.)

From left to right: Visitor from Chicago; Preston Thomas,
owner of the nearby Thomas Ranch; Unknown; Charles
W. Coe; Unknown; Henry "Harry" W. Coe, Jr.

(Photograph from the author's collection.)

What readers are saying

Whether you punch cattle or push paper,
chances are that you'll learn something
from Peter Coe Verbica's
Hard-Won Cowboy Wisdom.

"I'm 84 now and forever etched in my memory are the
honest,
hard-working, weathered old cowboys
of my youth. They took this tenderfoot
and through years of working cattle taught
me cattle-savvy and their codes for a happy life.
I am forever grateful to all of them. Peter pays them
their due respect."

James Harvey
Sundog Ranch,
Prescott, Arizona

"'Assume nothing,' but be sure to mine
Peter Coe Verbica's book.
You'll find some gold nuggets to
pass along to loved ones."

Dex Reeder
COC Ranch,
Harper, Oregon

"As someone who grew up with many
of the same cattlemen and riders over the years,
it's a pleasure to see Peter Coe Verbica bring
his *Hard-Won Cowboy Wisdom* to a wider audience."

Chris Lybbert
Pro Rodeo Hall-of-Famer,
World Title, All-Around Category, 1982,
World Title, Tie-down Roping, 1986
Lybbert Ranch
Forestberg, Texas

"A must-read with tremendous scope.
Peter Coe Verbica's *Hard-Won Cowboy Wisdom*
brings back memories of my own personal hunting
and ranch experiences. The book echoes
many of the lessons taught to me by my
dad and grandfather.

Jim Oneal
Isabel Valley Ranch,
Mt. Hamilton Range, California

"Country music is three chords and the truth."

Harlan Howard

Preface

At first glance, Peter C. Verbica does not appear to be the kind of man who would be an expert on cowboy lore. For one thing, he hardly ever appears in public without a tie. He writes in longhand using a fountain pen. His job has something to do with investments; he plays a lively game of tennis; and, he teaches a college class in his spare time. He is bespectacled instead of bronzed. You would not immediately associate him with tobacco products, saddle soap or a campfire. Rumor has it, he does slip into jeans and boots and disappears to a ranch in Wyoming from time to time, but I cannot personally confirm this.

What I can confirm is, Sherlock Holmes to the contrary, initial impressions can be deceiving. I had not known him an hour before he confessed he had grown up on a cattle ranch in the Santa Clara Valley. That gave me pause. I am a native of this same valley and I thought such things had all been turned into housing developments long before this lanky man with the infectious laughter came into this world. The truth is, he arrived during the Santa Clara Valley's transition from an entrepreneurial center for agriculture and ranching to the technology center known as Silicon Valley. An educated man from a family of educated ranchers, Peter was raised with a cowboy boot in one world and a wingtip shoe in the other.

The key to his cowboy *bona fides* can be found in his middle name—Coe. His great great grandfather Coe came to California at about the time of the Gold Rush and his great grandfather, Henry Willard Coe, established the Pine Ridge Ranch at the south end of San Francisco Bay in 1905. Those of you who know the region know that his family land, with its Coe heritage, is now a state park. Young Peter is one of the few among us who can say he was born and raised on a genuine California rancho.

There is something about the code of the American West—with its danger and its camaraderie and its good and evil characters—that appeals to people all over the world. The formula of a Western story attracts many of us with its sense of order and justice: hence the enduring popularity of Western movies. With this collection, author Peter Coe Verbica pays tribute to this universality. Here you will find wisdom in the simple truths uttered by those who may just see the world more clearly because they take their rest each night under a blanket of Western stars.

Robin Chapman
Los Altos, Calif.
October 2015

There's an old maxim that "nothing grows under the shade of large trees." Having successful ancestors is part of that profound and humbling reality. Rather than lament our limitations, I prefer to think that we should climb up among the branches of our families' histories and survey the breathtaking view. Let's build a treehouse above it all, keep our youthful enthusiasm, and throw dirt clods at the cynics below.

This small book of cowboy maxims and practical tips may not provide great amusement value; there is a remarkable absence of the coy and cute. I'm not Buffalo Bill and I apologize from the beginning for not producing a Wild West show and serving you popcorn. Most of the suggestions and observations are based on someone being killed or injured at worst, and being schooled with a memorable lesson at best. By and large, I've redacted

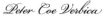

the names of those taught by the headaches and heart-aches, but I've kept their epiphanies intact.

Many of these suggestions are based on stories or events shared as part of my family's history in ranching (the Coe Brothers' ranch at Pine Ridge, timber holdings in Maine and New Hampshire, and *Rancho San Felipe* nestled in the foothills of California). But, I also owe a debt of gratitude to cattlemen, horse breakers, deer hunters, ranch hands and managers, who've offered their "two cents."

It's true that I am a zealous advocate of cowboy culture and rue, like many, a modern world where history is re-written, where up is down and down is up, where those who have no dog in the hunt seek to divide rather than harmonize. Eric Arthur Blair warned us much more eloquently of these risks, but this is my stake in the ground, my Western epistle to shield against the epithets, my book of hard-won cowboy wisdom.

Perhaps, if you can slug through a few of these pages, I can persuade you not to ride off into the sunset, but rather take the risk of returning to town, bruise a knuckle or two, and defend the honor of the West and those cowboys and cowgirls who went honorably before you.

And, as a reward (or punishment) for reading these aphorisms, I've included one of my cowboy poems, "I grew up" at the end of the collection. Like a strong cup of coffee, I think that the piece has its merits. Let me know if you agree or even if you don't.

Peter Coe Verbica
San Jose, Calif.

Other Works by the Author

Greece at Peace and Other Poems of Life, Love and Faraway Places

A Key to the Grove and Other Poems

Left at the Gate and Other Poems

Early photograph of Rancho San Felipe. Circa 1899.

(Photograph from the author's family's collection.)

Hard-Won
Cowboy Wisdom

(Not Necessarily in Order of Importance.)

1.

If you're the youngest, get the gate, do the dishes and
say "yes, sir" or "yes, ma'am."

2.

A dull knife is useless for skinning.

Winnifred Coe Verbica and Lucky
at Pine Ridge in the 1940's.

(Photograph from HWC [Jr.] State Park archives.)

3.

Never ask a cattleman how many head he's running, the number of acres of his spread, or the age of his wife or daughter.

4.

There are things that will gore you, stalk you, strike you, bite you, stomp you, buck you and kill you if you're stupid, so listen up.

5.

Loans can be very easy to get but very hard to pay off. Know what a "demand" note means versus a "term" note.

6.

A wife can be expensive, so watch how she spends before you marry.

7.

If you gamble, drink, smoke, chew or mess around too
much,
you will be poorer at best and poor at worst.

Ranch owner and philanthropist Sada Coe Robinson with
her granddaughter, Mae Lim Harrison, daughter of
Carmel artists, Irene "Renie" Robinson Lim
and Y.S. "Garlon" Lim.

Ms. Coe Robinson lived her later years on a
sprawling rural Mount Hamilton Road property with
an orchard, aviary and original wood stove in its kitchen.
She would enjoy an occasional "Old Fashioned" and steak
at the Grandview Restaurant which overlooked the
Santa Clara Valley.

A study in contrasts, Ms. Coe Robinson, nature lover,
amateur poet and cowgirl, also owned the "Carolands Chateau"
in Hillsborough, Calif., which is on the National Register of
Historic Places.

(Photograph from HWC [Jr.] State Park collection.
Courtesy of Teddy Goodrich.)

8.

You can learn a lot about a man by how he builds a
fence and treats his mother.

9.

Clean and oil your guns. You're just holding on to them
for the next generation.

10.

Just because you're the owner doesn't make you better.
The best owners know this truth.

Benny Nunes with dead mountain lion
at Pine Ridge.

11.

Quoting the Bible or a philosopher doesn't make you Godly or wise, but that doesn't mean you shouldn't read.

12.

Plant fruit trees, but plan for deer.

Snippet from Harry Coe's (HWC Jr.) diary
written in 1935 when he was 74
years of age at *Rancho San Felipe.*

13.

A good hunter doesn't shoot an animal just because it's legal; a good hunter doesn't mind passing on a smaller animal and waiting until next season.

14.

Writing a "thank you" note doesn't make you a sissy.

15.

Don't wear too big of a buckle unless you've earned it.

16.

Let the saw do the work.

17.

Learn how to rope and swing a hammer.

18.

If you can play a guitar, fiddle, banjo, harmonica, or sing on key, my hat's off to you.

19.

Have your property lines surveyed. You may be surprised one way or another.

20.

If you don't know what an easement, right-of-way, deed or lien is, learn.

21.

Make sure you save for property taxes.

22.

Never ever trust a politician, especially if he says that
he's a God-fearing one or an atheist.

23.

If you can make it or repair it yourself, there's a good
chance
that you'll save some money, or at least learn
something.

24.

Do your best not to make fun of newbies who close
a gate and realize that they're on the wrong side.

Charles W. Coe at Rancho San Felipe. Caption in family
photo album reads: "CWC dishing frijoles. Coffee 80 gallons.
Pit for roasting meat in background." Circa 1899.

(Photograph from the author's family's collection.)

25.

Go to church at least once a year. (The more often you go, the less troubled your sleep.)

26.

A real cowboy takes his hat off when entering someone's home and tips his hat to a lady.

27.

Take care of your saddles, boots and horses.

28.

When you ride, wear the right boots or risk getting dragged to death.

29.

Your horse will spook when you're least expecting it.

30.

Apologize to your parents and siblings for your stupidity as a child, even if you're certain that you did nothing wrong.

31.

When you need a gun the most is usually when you
don't have it.
The 750 pound boar I saw last was very happy I wasn't
carrying a rifle.

32.

Unpleasant things can happen to people who hang
around bars late at night.

33.

If you fix it with baling wire today, you'll be fixing it
again tomorrow.

(Or, as Paul Wenger's (of the Wenger Ranch) dad
taught him:

"A lazy man works twice as hard.")

34.

To lift a hay bale, use your knee.

35.

When you pass a neighbor on the road, wave.

36.

A wife who cuts your hair will save you money.

37.

Have a decent dentist and a good lawyer.

38.

Keep your barns clean.

39.

Try to hire honest hands and horse shoers, but invest in decent hinges and locks.

40.

Never buy a new car, truck, boat or plane, but have a mechanic who knows more than you inspect what you're buying.

41.

Don't force it. If you are, you're probably doing it wrong and will strip the threads.
(As Bill Storm used to joke, "Don't force it. Use a bigger hammer.")

42.

There's nothing sweeter than home-grown vegetables or a first kiss.

43.

Any man who kicks his dog isn't a man.

44.

Spay your cats.

45.

Try to set a good example for your children as best as you can.

46.

Every year is a chance for a fresh season.

47.

Rotate your crops.

48.

Don't overgraze.

49.

Write who people are under photographs for your great grandchildren's sake.

50.

Teach your daughters how to shoot.

Harry Coe (HWC Jr.) in his later years
at *Rancho San Felipe* on the
horse that he had saddled up every day, whether he
decided to go riding or not. Tapaderos helped with the
brush and weather.

(Photograph from the author's family's collection.)

51.

Make sure your son knows how to field dress an animal.

52.

Always be polite to the sheriff, ranger,
game warden, banker, butcher, and tax collector.

53.

Make sure your firebreaks are well-maintained.

54.

Never buy a cheap knife, gun, rod or watch,
unless you're prepared to throw it away.
Don't buy cheap paint, boots or tools either.

55.

Learn at least three good, clean jokes.

56.

Plan your estate well. Your government is rapacious
and unforgiving.

57.

Have a decent pantry.

58.

Your daughters should know how to can fruit and your sons should know how to dry fruit.

59.

The later the hour, the more drunks on road.

60.

Ride your fences.

61.

Don't over-grade your dirt roads unless you want to end up with a ravine later.

62.

Install culverts, stock ponds, tanks and springs.

63.

Beware of most people from town; they will vote your property rights out from under you and cost you more in the end than the boldest of thieves.

64.

Write down license plate numbers of unfamiliar vehicles
and don't hesitate to call the sheriff. Chances are that they're trespassing or up to no good.

65.

When you tie a dally, watch your fingers.

66.

If it's a long shot, adjust for the yardage.

67.

Always have a spare tire and jack, road flares and a couple of bottles of water.

68.

If you swear to God, you're undercutting your veracity.

69.

Save jam jars. They make decent glasses.

Pine Ridge Ranch.

(Photograph from the author's collection.)

70.

Mix some pork in with venison.

71.

The trick to great jerky is the cut of the meat.

72.

Learn how to build a decent fire and how to prevent one.

73.

Some people are just mean. Steer clear of them as best as you can.

74.

Know at least one decent tractor mechanic.

Haying season at *Rancho San Felipe*. Circa 1899.

(Photograph from author's family's collection.)

75.

Lube your tractors, balers, and mowers as required.

76.

There are very few things more upsetting than mowing the legs off of a fawn during hay season.

Suck it up as best you can.

77.

If you're not keen on being hired by anyone right away, consider a tattoo or piercing.

78.

If someone doesn't believe in his heart that the West is the best, do not trust him.

79.

Keep your finger out of the trigger guard until you are ready to shoot.

Heading out for a ride at Pine Ridge Ranch.

(Photograph from the author's collection.)

80.

A gun is always loaded, whether you think it is or not. Always check it.

81.

Never point a gun at something unless you're prepared to shoot it.

82.

Insurance is a racket, but make sure that you're adequately covered.

83.

Gut shots are messy; neck shots are cleaner and ruin
less meat.

84.

Don't over-tighten a barbed wire fence. Keep an old
boot with
staples and a hammer handy in your truck.

85.

Know how to tie a few decent knots, including a honda
for roping and a quick-release knot for hitching your
horse.

86.

Saddle bags are a decent investment, but
make sure that they're strapped down properly.

87.

Check your cinch.

88.

Don't let your horse graze while you are trail riding.
It's a bad habit for the horse and a worse one for the
rider.

89.

If you come upon a gate that's closed, CLOSE IT!

90.

There's nothing uglier than a cute kid swinging on a gate; he's just making sure that it will drag later.

91.

Don't drive off with a horse tied to your horse trailer.

92.

Don't use a rifle as a cane to help you get over
a fence, no matter how old you get, unless you're
interested in losing a finger or worse.

93.

Check your reins so that you're ready to control your
horse quickly if needed.

94.

Don't go off of the road unless absolutely necessary;
it wastes feed and a hot muffler can start a fire.

95.

Only an idiot drives fast around cattle and spooks them.

96.

Know at least one true story about a relative trying
to lasso a mountain lion, wrestling a buck bare-handed
or splitting a match with a revolver at fifty paces.

(My mom infamously tried to lasso a mountain lion
at Pine Ridge Ranch while on horseback.

Lumberman Bob Hoffmann, a giant of a man,
wrestled a buck bare-handed next to his
apple tree after cold cocking it with a brick.

My grandmother, Pat Coe, was known for being
a lady and splitting match sticks at remarkable
distances.)

97.

Labs are great for ducks but very bad for boar;
in a fight, a wild boar will kill a lab every time.
For boar, try a Queensland heeler.

98.

Keep a wood-stave water tank and water trough full.

99.

Cattle need mineral blocks and salt licks.

Winnifred Coe Verbica at Pine Ridge circa 1942.

(Photograph from author's family's collection.)

100.

Elk are tough on fences.

101.

A .357 Mag or a .40 isn't enough for a wild boar or a bear. Invest in a .44 Mag.

102.

Coyotes, wolves, wild dogs and lions kill calves and fawn.

103.

If a woman leaves your party nude,
you're picking the wrong guests
or serving way too much liquor.

104.

Having a knife clip show on the outside
of your pocket is an embarrassment, but having
a knife in your pocket is practical.

105.

Tell your kids not to put rocks down septic flues.

106.

Don't climb a willow tree. The branches break easily.

107.

You may have a great partner but get everything
in writing, because there are always wives and children.

108.

If you don't know what poison oak or poison ivy looks
like, I feel sorry for you.

109.

A branding isn't pretty.

110.

Get the door for your wife or daughter, even if she insists you not do so.

111.

Take pictures of your children doing things with you, like riding horses, hunting, fishing or camping. They need proof that they matter to you.

112.

If your wife insists on a divorce, do NOT beg her to stay. She is gone and most likely will never come back. Wish her well, try to keep what property you can, and never speak ill of her to your children. If you wait four years, she may want to come back, but at that point, the odds are you won't want her to.

113.

If one man tells you that real estate is better than stock, and another tells you that stock is better than real estate, and another tells you that bullion is better than stock or real estate, and another that owning a business is best, or yet another that bonds or cash is king, each will be right -- at some point in time.

114.

If you are looking to buy a ranch, find out about the water, the real reason it's for sale and don't pay too much. Watch out for underground storage tanks and their plumes.

115.

Walking and riding your property will keep you healthier.

116.

You will have plenty of friends if you let them hunt; but, true friends are more difficult to discern.

117.

Never get a personalized license plate.

118.

The wealthiest will often insist that they don't have any money.

119.

Don't crowd cattle on the road unless you want your truck door dented.

Cousins. From left to right: Caroline Verbica, Hannah Salters, Daniel Salters, Madeline Verbica, Esther Salters, David Salters, Elizabeth Verbica.

(Photograph from the author's collection.)

Madeline Verbica, Elizabeth Verbica
and Jake at the brick house.
Note the wild boar signs on the hillside.

(Photograph from the author's collection.)

Madeline Verbica, author, Vanessa Verbica, Elizabeth Verbica.

(Photograph from author's collection.)

Author and mother, Winnifred Coe Verbica.

(Photograph from author's family's collection.)

120.

Learn about U.S. history, including the history of ethnicities besides yours.

121.

The cowboy legacy is color-blind.

Don't be a racist, but beware those who think they have a moral high ground over others.

Human nature is such that whoever is in power will attempt to lord over others.

(Anyone who thinks cowboys were just of Northern European ancestry doesn't know much about the history of the West.)

122.

A dog who bites will bite again. Get rid of it.

123.

You could do worse than having some gold
or silver bullion or numismatic coins, but
keep in mind the high transaction costs if
you're buying at retail and having to sell at wholesale.

124.

Remember that even the toughest men
and most beautiful of women lose to Father Time,
so treat others with respect and don't take flattery too
seriously.

Hank Coe (HSC) with horse. *Rancho San Felipe.*
Circa 1935.

(Photograph from the author's family's collection.)

125.

Knowing how to fish is a necessity.

126.

Even if you think you know a better way,
if you're the new kid, hold off on your opinion
until your boots are broken in.

127.

Remember that a semiautomatic throws
another round in the chamber. Just because
the magazine is out, doesn't mean that there
isn't a round in the chamber.

128.

Teach your children firearm safety when they are young.

129.

Invest in a decent gun safe.

130.

Make sure you have a backstop before you shoot.

131.

Don't trot or gallop your horse toward the barn.

132.

Ground squirrels are a menace to cattle and horses' hooves.

133.

If you're a woman and want a handgun for self-protection, buy a snub-nose .38 and practice with it. A longer barreled pistol is more likely to be grabbed away from you. If it's hammerless, you can pull it out of a holster, pocket or purse faster.

134.

Don't fire a weapon near someone else's ear.

135.

Wear ear protection when using a larger caliber weapon.

136.

Wear appropriate glasses when shooting.

137.

When in rattlesnake country, wear high top boots.

138.

Let others know where you're heading before leaving the ranch house in case you don't come back.

139.

Try not to drive dirt roads when they're muddy. You'll create ruts and worse yet, may get stuck.

140.

A bone saw will save you time. Invest in a couple.

141.

A steel and portable sharpener will make butchering easier.

142.

Keep your waterproof flashlight freshly charged and always have it with you.

143.

You can make a canteen out of a gallon jug, gunny sack and baling twine; tie it to the back of your truck's cab. Wetting the gunny sack will keep it cool as the water evaporates.

144.

If you give the county road crew a cold case of beer, they may pave your private driveway for free.

145.

You will see more wildlife on a horse than by walking, but make sure your horse is trained properly before firing a weapon off it or near it.

146.

Put mosquito fish in your horse troughs and stock
ponds.

147.

If permitted, periodically burn your dump rubbish
down
when the season is right, but beware of fire.

148.

Painting the underside of porch eaves a light blue
will cut down on swallows building mud nests.

149.

Over-spec a bit when you build. There's nothing wrong with building something that's sturdy.

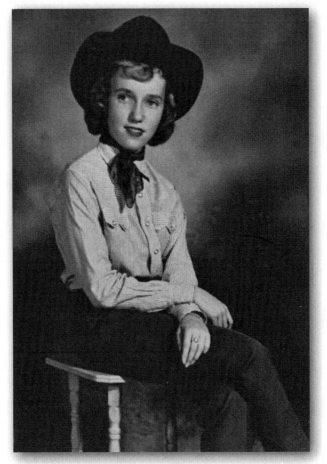

(Portrait of Winnifred Coe Verbica as a young teen.)

(Photograph from the author's family's collection.)

150.

If you don't want bored kids, build a swimming hole
and install a rope swing.

151.

Teach your children not to put bacon grease down the
sink drain.

152.

A wormwood bath provides a home remedy
analgesic for poison oak rash, but you may want
to read up on wormwood before trying it. I took one
such baths when I was a kid and survived.

153.

Don't use bottles for target practice unless you're prepared to pick up all of the glass.

154.

Buy blue chip stocks (or funds)
and reinvest your dividends
and capital gains.
Encourage your children to try this early on.

155.

Watch out for hobby loss rules; you could be
in for a big tax bill if your losses are disallowed
later; discuss this with your CPA.

156.

Setting a deeper well next to your neighbor's
will not earn you any friends, especially if
you're pulling for irrigation and he needs the water for
his house.

157.

Put a cattle guard across your neighbor's easement
and you'll wind up in court if he needs to drive
his herd through your property, especially if he
has had a long history of doing so.

158.

Don't lick your fingers and learn how to set a table.

159.

If you have an old truck or jeep, remember to take
the wheels out of four-wheel drive
before you get back on the road. If you forget,
you could end up seriously damaging your vehicle.

160.

Drinking and horseback riding don't mix well.

161.

Drink after you hunt, not before.

162.

A horse is easier to train when he's a colt.
So's a dog that's a pup.

163.

Outdoor cats will help keep down your barn mice.

164.

A willow switch is a cruel but effective instructor
with children and if ever used, should be used
very sparingly and for an extraordinarily good reason.

165.

Keep a Jeep or truck angled straight up or down on a
steep hill, not sideways, so that you don't roll it
and kill yourself or your passengers. This goes the
same for tractors.

166.

Slow down before a sharp curve, especially if you're in
a Jeep.

167.

Try not to burp or make other inappropriate noises in
front of a lady.

168.

Do not play cards or dice for high stakes, ever.

169.

Stay out of fights, but learn how to box. Make sure to calmly remove your tie and glasses.

170.

Trim branches on favorite trails every once in a while.

171.

Never litter.

172.

Railroad tie gate posts will last a long time.

173.

Whitewash your buildings, gates and board fences.
They'll last longer.

174.

Clean your chimney and laundry flues.

175.

Bake a pie for a new neighbor.

176.

Take dancing lessons and walk with your wife.

177.

There's nothing wrong with tapaderos. They
force you to ride on the balls of your feet
and if you're naive enough to wear the wrong shoes,
they'll save your life.

178.

Learn some Spanish -- and not just swear words
from the ranch hands.

179.

Summon all of your courage and get a pedicure at least
once.

180.

Have your children hoe the weeds down around your barns. It will let them build some calluses and keep them out of trouble for a while.

181.

Build a smaller home than you can afford, but make sure there's room where you can expand later as needed. You'll pay less in property taxes in the meantime.

182.

Go to college or vocational school and get your degree
or certificate.

183.

Wear a seatbelt.

184.

An angry woman with a gun is a dangerous
combination.
I know two ranch managers who can attest to this fact
first hand.

185.

Don't crack your knuckles.

186.

Don't use oleander branches for s'mores or hot dogs.
It will kill you.

187.

Wrap your outdoor pipes with gunny sacks;
it can help keep the pipes from freezing.

188.

When pulling hay bales from the barn, watch out for
black widows.
Use buckskin gloves.

189.

If your horses are chewing on their stalls or fences,
they probably need pasturing and exercise.

190.

The sharper the spurs, more than likely, the duller the
rider.

191.

Carry toilet paper. You'll regret not having any if you're on a long ride.

This is perhaps more important than the old cowboy adage, "Don't squat with your spurs on."

192.

If slicing an apple, don't aim the point of the knife towards your palm.

193.

Don't make fun of the "C" student.
You may end up having to work for him someday.

194.

Send care packages to U.S. troops and include
hand-written cards from grammar school children.

195.

Put a large donkey in with your horses to help protect
them from mountain lions.

196.

Geese will help keep the insects down around ranch houses.

197.

If you have a center-fire rig, consider a double cinch rig instead.

198.

Proper stirrup length should allow you to stand up with about a fist's distance between your rump and the saddle.

199.

If you're doing steep trail riding, consider a
breast-collar.

200.

Don't hang on to your horn if your horse gets out of
control. Get control of your reins. If your horse won't
stop, pull a single rein hard and deliberately towards
your knee and into the side of the horse. But, not too
quickly or you may pull off the bridle.

201.

Consider the source when a trainer is selling
you a horse. Her high opinion of the horse
most likely will wane significantly if you
ever try to sell it back to her. (Yes, this is based
on personal experience.)

202.

An old cowboy used to ask me if I'd ever amount to
much. After having years to think about this, I believe in my bones that you and I amount to something
already.

203.

Grapes attract yellow jackets and wasps. You can kill them both by hanging a chunk of fatty meat on a string in a suspended jar and putting oil at the bottom. The wasps eat until they're full and then fall into the oil and can't swim out.

There are other variations to this approach using water, sugar, vinegar and other concoctions but you may risk killing helpful bees.

204.

Planting a rosebush at the end of your vineyard may give you an early warning when bad fungi strike.

205.

Cougar tracks usually don't show the nails unless they're in mud or snow. Mountain lion tracks in dust can be more difficult to identify because the weight is often on the back pad. (Look for the third lobe in the middle bottom of the back pad.)

I've seen a lion running with a distressed and very vocal piglet in its mouth. This was in the hillside field in back of the brick colonial home where my sister and I grew up (the same one where we were stalked by a lion as children in our yard).

Once, a sow and her piglets ran just in front of our Jeep. They were being chased by a mountain lion which was so tired that it laid down right next to us panting. It took off a few moments later. My dad and I enjoyed that incredible moment with a chuckle.

206.

Don't put your eye socket too close to your scope.
You could end up with a messy and painful lesson.

207.

To avoid injury, don't put your thumb or other part of
your hand directly in the semi-automatic pistol's slide
action plane when you're ready to fire.

208.

"Buck fever" is a real phenomenon. A novice hunter
may throw out live cartridges rather than firing them,
fire near too close to other hunters and other zany
antics. This was one of my dad's rueful stories after
taking a bunch of city slickers hunting. An experienced
guide with a calm voice helps the novice to take it
down a notch and think more clearly.

209.

Keep your water tank, wells and crawl spaces rodent
proof.
It's unpleasant to discover a dead squirrel floating in
your water tank.

210.

Redwood lasts longer than pine.

211.

Riding a well-trained cutting horse is pure joy.
The slightest signal from the rider brings
about a quick response.

212.

When you're walking, look down from time to time for snakes, especially around logs.

213.

Unfenced mine shafts are the bane of deer and curious children.

214.

A bottle of whiskey can kill a horse with colic.
(I won't name the cattleman who found this out.)
You're best off talking with your vet when you have a sick animal.

215.

Slow down for blind curves. Not everyone drives as well as you do. I've known those who've endured a head-on collision on a country road who can attest to this.

216.

An isolated country road can be an invitation for trouble. I've come across a stolen safe dumped down a canyon, a bad motorcycle accident, gang members and a murder victim. I know others who've discovered suicides and illegal pot growers and their garbage. If you're not an advocate of the Second Amendment, you're naïve.

217.

One way to cut down on trouble is to have a ranch hand deputized by the Sheriff or allow a retired or off-duty police officer hunt your property.

218.

Remote cameras can help identify thieves.

219.

If you have permission and must smoke out on a trail
in the summer, find a clearing without dry grass, and
spit into the palm of your hand to douse the remaining
embers of your filter-less cigarette. But, remember that
a number of the cowboys who modeled for tobacco ads
subsequently died of lung cancer.

Elizabeth Verbica heading up to the Isabel Valley Ranch, circa 2015.

(Photograph from the author's collection.)

220.

I always admired my grandfather's tour d' force of
not bothering with a spittoon while he played cards.
I didn't inherit this particular variety of intestinal
fortitude.

221.

If you have ranch accounts at the feed and hardware
stores and extend charging privileges to your workers,
be prepared to review the charges.

222.

You would be hard-pressed to improve on Roy Rogers'
prayer.

223.

If you stay awake during the sermon or homily, you'll make friends with at least two people: the reverend (or pastor) and your spouse.

224.

Buzzards circling overhead do imply a carcass.

225.

If you see an area that looks as if it's been gone over with a rototiller or there are oak trees painted with mud, chances are that wild boar have been present.

226.

If you're in bear country, at a minimum have bear spray ready.

227.

A mountain lion will decimate a pen of sheep.

228.

Camouflage and a caller or two help when hunting wild turkeys.

229.

Pass on re-tread tires.

230.

A gate built so that you can open it from a horse is a beautiful thing.

231.

If you're bucked off and haven't broken anything or suffered a concussion, get back in the saddle.

232.

If you're riding in flash-flood, desert country
and a lightning storm strikes, you've
got two sets of problems. Getting down in a
gulley and you risk getting washed away.
Being the highest object and you risk getting
struck by lightning.

233.

Never lean your rod or rifle against a truck.

(Courtesy of Johnny Mac McNicholas.)

234.

Hearing a wounded boar breathing in high grass or chemise brush is guaranteed to make the hair stand up on the back of your neck.

If you're without a .44 handgun at the time, you'll be shopping for one -- if you survive the ordeal unscathed.

235.

A cattleman won't volunteer advice because he doesn't want to start a fight or have you quit the job.   So, if you're not sure about how to do something, ask.

236.

If you wear work boots, you may prefer a steel toed boot. If you're doing electrical work, you'll prefer something in a non-conductive composite. Remember that there can be capacitors which can still hold a charge even if the power is off.

237.

One way to talk a depressed cowboy out of suicide when he is sitting at a ranch table with a pistol and a bowl of coffee in front of him is to ask him not to because you would be stuck cleaning up the mess. He may feel sympathy for your plight and hand you the gun. (This is based on a true story.)

238.

Giving your in-laws paid-for dancing lessons for Christmas will stand you in good stead with your mother-in-law. But, your father-in-law may remark, "I thought that you liked me..." (You and your wife can sign up as well to show that you're being a good sport.)

239.

A chain saw and skill saw are not toys.
They can jump and do other nasty tricks.
Read up on safety precautions.

240.

ATVs can be dangerous. If you look up "moron" in the dictionary, don't be surprised to see a picture of an ATV rider going too fast, not wearing a helmet, with a passenger, sporting a short-sleeve shirt and driving on a paved road.

241.

Don't lean firewood against a ranch house.
Store it off of the ground and keep it covered.

242.

You can test firewood for being too green by banging it
together; if it's green, it will make a "thud" sound. If it's
dry and seasoned, it will ring when struck together.

243.

Wet hay bales can cause spontaneous combustion.

244.

Tea tree oil concoctions reportedly help repel fleas and ticks.

245.

Pack a decent first aid kit.

246.

Teach your children to swim at a young age.

247.

Pack some extra shells in your pocket in case you miss.

248.

Reading the Constitution, Bill of Rights, Declaration of Independence and the Federalist Papers doesn't make you a kook. It makes you a patriot.

249.

City slicker: How many cows are you running?

Cattleman: Just enough to keep me out of trouble.

250.

A decent ranch gelding is virtually priceless.

251.

Don't flash cash or jewelry at the saloon if you're new in town. You could end up rolled in the alley.

252.

Finish what you start, but think first about what you're starting.

253.

If you make a promise, be prepared to keep it.

254.

A handshake from an honest man is worth more than an iron-clad contract with a grifter.

"Bosco" Verbica taking a break at the top of the Coe Ranch.
Some years he would shoot over 70 wild boar and donate
the meat to charity and friends.

Known for his booming voice, if he liked
a church choral performance, he would often yell "Bravo!"
Most parishners didn't know that he
bought the donuts on his own
dime behind the scenes for two to three services each weekend
for decades. To supply the high volume, he would have to drive
to multiple donut shops.

His other favorite pastime was surprising friends and
strangers at local coffee shops who,
when going to pay their bill,
would find out that it had already been
taken care of by Mr. Verbica.

255.

Ride for the brand.

(Translation: Don't bite the hand that feeds you.)

Courtesy of Dex Reeder.

256.

A cowboy who talks less often says more.

Ranch hand Al Gomez drawn in 1956 by Nancy Coe.

Nancy Coe's paintings of her grandfather, HWC, Jr.
and aunt, Sada Coe Robinson,
can be seen at the Pine Ridge ranch museum
at Henry Coe State Park in Morgan Hill, Calif.

(From the author's collection.)

257.

Remember that there are some things which aren't for sale.

258.

To be successful, be prepared to fail.

259.

Most teenage boys do think about just one thing.

260.

Be prepared to do what needs to be done, like putting down your favorite horse or dog.

261.

A horse trader may dope a jittery horse to make it appear calm.

262.

If you know about the Bill Pickett Incident, you're officially a cowboy trivia nerd. If you have the error proof sheet featuring his brother, Ben, and the corrected proof featuring Bill, you're a cowboy wonk like me.

263.

Make sure a buck is dead before throwing it into your
Jeep.
(Slit the windpipe.)

264.

A plastic tarp cuts down on the mess.

265.

Horse hair cinches made of mane are usually the best.

Eucalyptus tree at *Rancho San Felipe* which
fell over and narrowly missed
killing HWC, Jr. Circa 1925. In later years, I had to have
the ranch's blacksmith shop repaired
after a similar incident damaged
the building.

(Photograph from the author's collection.)

266.

Eucalyptus trees have shallow roots and when they fall can damage ranch buildings or worse.

267.

If you don't have time to run cattle full-time, consider leasing or licensing the grazing rights.

268.

Depending on your circumstances and school district, consider home-schooling your children, but try to have them do team sports if possible.

269.

Visit your family's gravesite every once in a while out of respect to those who've gone before you and to remember where you came from.

(I had information included on the master headstone for close family buried or interred elsewhere as a courtesy to the next generation. Make sure the stonecutter leaves enough room for the margins.)

270.

If you can't put down the bottle, meet with a friend of
Bill W.
If you have a loved one who can't put down the bottle,
meet with a friend of Lois W.

271.

Running out of gas and flying in weather or conditions
above your pay grade are two common causes of
small plane crashes. Ask if your bush pilot has a current
instrument rating, check the weather, and then the call
is up to you.

One incident where a small plane crashed on a ranch
involved de-icing the plane's windshield with a cup of
warm tea. On take-off, the tea re-froze, completely
eliminating visibility. The pilot over-compensated and
pulled the plane up too fast out of concern for power-lines
and a tree line. The plane stalled and went down nearly
nose first.

272.

Encourage your son to become an Eagle Scout.

(Ben Coe, great, great grandson of Charles W. Coe,
is working on his Eagle Scout project which involves
the Coe brothers' former Pine Ridge Ranch,
now part of Henry Coe State Park.)

273.

If you have guests and a decent spread or a lot to lose, consider a release, waiver of liability, assumption of risk and indemnity agreement; consult an attorney who knows what she's doing.

274.

Let your children buy some of their school clothes with their summer ranch wages.

275.

Don't run too many steers on the first day of break-
ing in a new rope. To break in a new rope, you can put
it on a post or a tree with the honda up and stretch it
with the weight of your body a few times.

276.

A respectable roping dummy, saddle, cowboy hat, belt
buckle, rope, hunting knife, lever-action rifle, or pair
of roping boots is bound to put a dirt-eating grin on a
young cowboy's face at Christmas.

277.

Take the length and slack out of your rope in the branding corral as a courtesy.

278.

Training a cutting horse in a hot, enclosed horse barn can involve a lot of galloping at full tilt, stopping, starting and spinning in heavy dust.

279.

Usually deer are fairly skittish, but if you encounter a buck at close range while walking and it isn't startled by you, calmly keep your distance. It may be preoccupied by a doe or looking warily at your dog. Not to be shrill, but the buck has a full rack of horns and you don't.

(I just got back from a walk with my wife and we encountered a nice three-pointer which wouldn't budge from the trail. He had a doe in the brush, was busy sniffing the ground and finally sauntered off. Refer to #31.)

"Winnie" Coe Verbica grinning atop a heifer calf
at Pine Ridge, circa 1942.

*(Photograph from the HWC [Jr.] State Park
archives courtesy of Teddy Goodrich.)*

280.

Teach your young children not to approach strange dogs willy-nilly (i.e., with their face close to the animal's muzzle).

Ask the owner about the dog's demeanor first no matter how cute the pet looks.

281.

Unattended children are guaranteed to do interesting things.

When I was a toddler, my parents found me a half a mile away in a red jumpsuit, surrounded by bulls with our yellow Lab calmly sitting next to me. When I was a little bit older, a school chum and I managed to cover the entire side of an out-building with nails while our parents were enjoying cocktails. I also had a habit of climbing up on three and four story high barn roofs in my pre-teens.

282.

If you live in earthquake country or are just
plain cautious, have two large trash cans full of food
and beverage staples which will last two years. At the
end of one year, donate the contents of one trash can to
a food bank and re-stock. If you want, you can also buy
a higher-quality water filter used for camping to help
ensure that you have access to potable water.

283.

If you know of an efficient and non-toxic way
of killing ground squirrels, you may persuade a
ranch owner or two to let you hunt his property.

284.

Rolled aluminum gates don't hold up too well,
even if they are light and easy to hang.

285.

To open a barbed wire and post gate
(sometimes referred to as a "Portagee Gate") put your
shoulder behind the fence post adjacent to the gate,
grab the first post in the gate and pull it towards you.
You'll create enough play to allow you to flip the
wire catch off of the gate.

287.

Don't set a rifle's muzzle directly on the floor of your Jeep or in the dirt.

288.

When setting a post, use an iron tamping iron bar to compress the dirt.

289.

When you offer your arm to your wife, walk on the side closest to the street.

290.

Barn flies are a pain. Fly predators, attractants, traps, air doors and industrial bug zappers with UV lures help.

291.

You can catch a gopher by turning over a gallon milk jug or five gallon water bottle into the hole. When the gophers try to escape, they swim into the milk jug or water bottle.

You can also set rat traps baited with peanut butter and sunflower seeds and cover the gopher or squirrel hole with a bucket.

Others use industrial rodent killer kits using flammable gas (i.e., a mixture of propane and oxygen).

Years ago, we were allowed poisoned grain for ground squirrels.

And, of course, there are always long guns.

292.

Give a horse's hind end an appropriate distance so that
you don't get kicked.

293.

I've heard the quote that "behind every rancher is a wife who works in town." I think that it's very fair to say that a rancher or farmer who has additional assets, income or business interests has an advantage over others who don't in the long run.

When foreign sovereigns or foreign entities tie up ranching, timber, farm property or Ag businesses, that's interesting (and potentially troubling) to me. I can cite many examples worldwide, including one which involves over 7.4 million acres of farmland, but will hold my tongue.

294.

I'll trade you ten cowboy quips for one practical suggestion on how to lift something heavy and not get a hernia.

295.

Your wife will ask you to hang the heaviest mirror and want it centered in the softest drywall. Find the wall studs with a magnet and run a tie board so that you
have something solid to attach the hardware.

296.

I wouldn't buy a Henry with John Wayne's picture on it, but I would buy a Henry.

297.

If there's enough at stake and enough cash flow from the real estate, an UPREIT structure may help you postpone recognition of capital gains, liquidate partners who want out and allow you to maintain control. Discuss this with a decent securities lawyer.

298.

Private equity managers understand meaning of "Two and Twenty." Even if it's not appropriate for you, it will help you understand how some fortunes are made.

299.

Grain silos can be dangerous and safety protocols should be encouraged and followed. Watch out for spoiled grain or grain which is too moist.

300.

Eat the game you kill.

301.

Have somebody hold your ladder, whether you think you need him to or not.

(Courtesy of "Johnny Mac" McNicholas)

302.

The best cure for a resentment is to take
off your boots, sit down and write
out a gratitude list. It will save you
having to make amends.

303.

A kid catching a ride on a Case steam tractor is one
happy kid.

304.

If your daughter is in the Navy, buy her a 1911 .45
with her strike fighter squadron's logo and
motto engraved on the grip and slide.

"RAM ON!"

305.

Don't be too proud to copy what your neighbor does,
but try to make it better.

(Courtesy of Barry Swenson.)

306.

If you think that you're the best rancher or farmer,
watch out.
You could be ready for a fall.

(Courtesy of Barry Swenson.)

307.

Hire hands who are recommended by people you trust.

(Courtesy of Barry Swenson.)

308.

Invite your neighbors to help at your brandings and feed them well afterward.

309.

Never let your kids tie their rope to a saddle's horn.

(Courtesy of Pearle Salters.)

310.

Don't lead a horse into a horse trailer to avoid getting stomped. Use the halter rope from the side. If the horse doesn't want to be trailered, you can tie another rope to one side of the trailer, lay the rope down and use it to guide the horse in from its back legs.

(Courtesy of Finn Jenssen.)

311.

If your horse stops to drop some road apples, let it finish.

If your horse stops on a trail for another reason, it may be because it's noticed a rattler before you have.

312.

A "running iron" is a bar with a hook at the end which when heated allows you to draw your brand.

(Courtesy of Jim Harvey.)

313.

A *riata* (or "gut line") is stiffer than a "seago" and better for roping.

(Courtesy of Jim Harvey.)

314.

In the old days, cowboys would carry bedrolls made
out of blue jeans and stuffed with cotton.

(Courtesy of Jim Harvey.)

315.

Wild dogs will kill a cow's calf and chew a cow's ears
off. Wild Bill Storm from Prescott roped a bunch of
wild dogs which did this and killed them one by one
with his pocket knife. He went back with a 30-30 and
killed three more.

(Courtesy of Jim Harvey.)

316.

An estate can bring out the worst in people. Remember that no matter what, your family members are more important than property or things. You don't have to forget, but do your best to forgive. Worry about keeping your side of the street clean.

317.

Don't startle a sleeping horse by approaching it from behind.

(Courtesy of Finn Jenssen.)

318.

Old cowboys know more than they let on,
but often won't tell you how to do something
in belief that you'll remember something better
if you learn from your own mistakes.

319.

Old cowboys were creative and would make use
of what was available, especially if it was free.
At the Sundog Ranch in Prescott, they would build
"slab" corrals, which were constructed from the
free slabs given to them from the lumber mill
after logs were milled.

(Courtesy of Jim Harvey.)

320.

If you're throwing big calves at a branding,
be careful to watch if the heeler lets up on the slack.
If the calf gets loose and starts circling
the header's horse, you could get slammed into
forcefully by the calf.

321.

A lower heartbeat and excellent eyesight can make
for a better shooter. A deer and a wolf have been
shot by an Enfield 30-06 at a half a mile by Bill Storm.

(Courtesy of Jim Harvey.)

322.

Watch out for old ammunition. When Bill Storm fired a 30-06 1914 Enfield WWI Army rifle (bought for $5 from the NRA by his step-son Jim Harvey), the mercuric primer ate the brass and it blew. Bill had gunpowder peppered in his cheek until the day he died; luckily he was wearing glasses when he fired the Enfield.

(Courtesy of Jim Harvey.)

323.

In country where it gets cold in the winter,
you'll have to break the ice in the water troughs
each day so that the animals can drink.

324.

In rocky country, some breeds of cattle's hooves are too
soft.

(Courtesy of Jim Harvey.)

325.

On an old Winchester Model 94 (like the one
Bill Storm bought brand new in 1924 for $21),
be careful that the hammer safety isn't set
too far back, because it will fire. If you want
to be safer, don't ride with one in the pipe.

(Courtesy of Jim Harvey.)

326.

A .460 Weatherby has a big kick. When
a hunter was asked why he didn't take
the shot at a deer, he replied, "After you've shot
this gun once, you think twice about shooting it again."

(Courtesy of Jim Harvey.)

327.

When pulling a calf, push the leg back
in and put your fingers into the nostrils
and under the bottom of the calf's chin and pull
it straight out. Make sure that the calf's legs
are together.

(Courtesy of Jim Harvey.)

328.

If you want to improve the accuracy of
your shooting, you can modify the
front and back sites of your 30-30.
If you're too good of a shot, they'll ban you
from the turkey shoot.

(Courtesy of Jim Harvey.)

329.

In the old days, when they had single-cylinder water pumps, you had to be careful. When the cylinder backfired, the pump jack would dislocate your thumb.

(Courtesy of Jim Harvey.)

330.

If you encounter a calf with a swollen head
and is nearly unrecognizable, it's been bitten by a
rattler.

(Courtesy of Jim Harvey.)

331.

In the old days, cowboys would get honey out
of Arizona oaks by cutting it with an ax. They'd
button their collars up tight because the bees weren't
happy about it.

(Courtesy of Jim Harvey.)

332.

When you shoe a horse, be sure to cut
and crimp the horse shoe nails one at a time. If you
wait to crimp the nails all at once, if the horse kicks,
you can end up with a nail driven clear through
your knuckle.

(Courtesy of Jim Harvey.)

333.

Be careful using a hand grinder with thin
metal; if it seizes, it can jump, rip through your palm
and you'll wind up with 18 stitches.

(Courtesy of Jim Harvey.)

334.

If you don't want to end up with a concussion,
don't throw rocks at bats in a barn when you're a kid.

335.

Cows will get ruptured teats if they lose a calf.
In the old days, they used turkey quills to drain the teat.

(Courtesy of Jim Harvey.)

337.

A saddle scabbard will wear the bluing off of your 30-30 over time. A work gun isn't for show. It's for getting the job done.

338.

If you surprise a thief, be prepared to be shot at. My great grandparent's house still has the evidence in its hall floorboards. If you're unarmed, your best option could be to run as fast as you can.

339.

A hungry mountain lion will try to break into
a house at night, so have a shotgun ready.

(This is based on a true story.)

340.

A good poem, like life,
doesn't always have to rhyme.

Here's something that I wrote which I like
from "The Ascension" in *A Key to the Grove*:

We pull the line with a wheel tractor,

and sink the metal jaws,
set the spring trap
into each bale and launch them up
four stories high.

And when a bale rises up
on twisting rope
and enters the barn doors,

and you stare into the midday sun,

silently smiling
in your own salt and stink,

it is as beautiful as
the Ascension.

340.

A pet monkey is adorable when it tucks a house cat
to bed, but it may run out of luck if caught trying
to smoke your favorite pipe. (My great grandfather got
rid of his pet monkey after this happened.)

341.

A kid won't sleep easily in an old ranch house
if told about a relative who died in the same guest
room.

342.

To a young child, nothing makes more noise at night than the ticking of a grandfather clock in a large room.

343.

You're a cowboy if you miss the smell of horse manure or the sound of coyotes howling. Or cattle lowing at night.

344.

Fencing both sides of your driveway will save
you from having to open and close your gate
if you have cattle in the same field where your
home is located. Your wife will be happy.

345.

To see if someone is flinching before they squeeze
the trigger, give them an empty gun and tell them
that it's loaded before they take a shot at a target.

346.

Don't leave a dog or small child locked alone
in the cab of your truck, even if you think you'll
only be gone for a minute.

347.

Return ranch tools to their rightful place, unless you
enjoy being yelled at.

348.

Clean up your job-site.

349.

Don't divulge your secret fishing spots.

350.

Don't stand up in a small boat (unless you're
George Washington and can get away with it).

351.

Pay attention to the bank and your footing when you're fly fishing if you're wearing waders or you could drown. If the bank gives way or you lose your footing, you can be pulled down by the current.

(Courtesy of Marcus Ervin.)

A fisherman I know of went down under eight feet of water, had to hold his breath, walk on the river bank and get to the other side. He made it. Another fisherman who wasn't as lucky was dragged into the current, got stuck under a log and died.

Deep water and rapids require increased vigilance.

Double-belting your waders tight can help. It's also been suggested to have a Coast Guard-approved CO_2 inflatable life vest and wear it properly.

352.

Don't lean back on a chair in the cookhouse.
If it's older wood or you're too heavy, you'll
end up on the floor embarrassed and shelling
money out for a new chair. (And, it's bad manners.)

353.

Board and batten siding make for handsome barns.

354.

Praying out loud with your spouse from
time-to-time can let you face challenges together
without your loved one feeling criticized.

355.

Teach your children not to dive into a shallow river
or creek.
The consequences can be permanent.

356.

You can get some insight into the integrity of
a hillside by looking at stress cracks in the pavement.

357.

Keep your vehicles locked around small children.
Walk around your vehicle to ensure that there
are no small children present. A rearview camera can
save a life and increase visibility, especially with a truck
or SUV.

358.

An automated external defibrillator ("AED") on the ranch can help save a life.

359.

A tilting retaining wall is under significantly more stress than one at a normal angle.

(Author's oldest daughter, Vanessa Coe Verbica, riding in
a hunter-jumper competition on German warmblood Sterling.
Vanessa would later serve for 5.5 years in the USN.)

(Photograph © by C. Cammett. Author's collection.)

360.

Have a barrier around your ranch's pool and a pool alarm.

361.

You can preserve your view of cattle and horses in pastures by using a "ha-ha" fence at your homestead.

(This trick was used by landscape designer Thomas Church.)

362.

If you have a chain across a fence opening, hang reflectors.

363.

Pulling porcupine barbs from a dog's muzzle takes focus and a pair of pliers.

364.

To keep from getting T-boned on a country road, inset the gate far enough to allow you to pull your truck and trailer off of the road.

365.

Don't let your children shoot up road signs, reflectors, or electric line insulators, capacitors, fuses or regulators.

366.

An electric fence can help keep wild boar out
of a vineyard or your yard.

367.

If you have an electric gate at your ranch or farm,
make sure that you install safety sensors.

368.

You can fix a sagging gate without having
to re-set the post by installing a small wheel at the
end of the gate.

369.

If the ground is too rocky, you can build a
buck or jackleg fence, but watch out for wind.
You can support it with additional rock.

370.

Don't pen horses with barbed wire.

371.

Shooting a Desert Eagle .50 is fun, but hold it firmly.
Limp-wrist the weapon and you could end up denting
your forehead.

372.

Hold a heavier gauge shotgun with the butt
of the gun pressed firmly against your shoulder,
your cheek against the stock and put your weight
on your front foot; keep your elbows bent; and, take
shooting lessons from someone who's well-trained and
cares about your safety.

373.

Varmints, such as muskrats, can burrow into levies and lake sides and impact their integrity. (This information is courtesy of the owner of bucolic Little Creek Farm.)

374.

Have a tailor deepen the inside pocket of your dress and work coats so that your wallet seats better. Add a flap and button if absent so that your wallet is less likely to fall out while galloping.

375.

Purchase electrical cords with a GFI (Ground Fault Circuit Interrupter) built in. (It's safer than just jury-rigging extension cord ends on a paint bucket with painter's tape.)

376.

Someone I know (who shall remain nameless) managed
to drive a perfectly good (but borrowed) truck
into a stump hidden by grass in the middle of a prairie;
extensive repairs were needed, reinforcing the maxim:

"Don't lend your truck out and don't borrow a truck
either."

(Maxim courtesy of Rich Carpenter.)

377.

Fly an American flag on your farm.

378.

Lunge a colt in a round pen before throwing a saddle on it; this will save you from being sore later.

379.

Preg-test with ultrasound. It's more accurate the old manual alternative, faster, cheaper in the long run and stresses your cows less.

(Courtesy of Dex Reeder.)

Pearle Verbica Salters heading a steer at
Rancho San Felipe (Coe Ranch).

(Photograph courtesy of Pearle Verbica Salters.)

380.

In the old days, in the high desert, Washoe Indian cowboys would use Yerba Mansa-based concoctions to deal with cuts and abrasions.

(Courtesy of Dex Reeder.)

381.

In the desert, pack a hoof pick to take care of rocks.

(Courtesy of Dex Reeder.)

382.

First thing when you show up at a party, figure
out where the back door is and make sure that your
truck has an unobstructed exit.

(Courtesy of Dex Reeder.)

383.

Burning Yucca cacti was a way that old time Indian
cowboy Duggan would mark a trail in the high desert
to mark the trail for the wranglers left behind and who
were driving stragglers from the herd.

(Courtesy of Dex Reeder.)

384.

If your horse tenses up with its ears pricked up and its nostrils blowing, watch out. You may have a bear ahead.

(Courtesy of Dex Reeder.)

385.

If you're riding at 11,000 feet, don't push your horse too hard.

(Courtesy of Dex Reeder)

386.

Properly winterize your cabin and if possible,
set it up so that you can drain your water heater and
pipes.

387.

Some are called. Keep the legacy of the West and cowboy culture alive.

If you donate a ranch or conservation rights make sure
that you hire a decent lawyer; in a well-crafted and
durable document which runs with the land, require
that the subsequent stewards, whether public or private, allow for prudent cattle grazing, hiking, fishing,
horseback riding, hunting, prudent timber harvesting,
reasonable mineral, oil and gas and water rights management, and ranch infrastructure maintenance and
expansion, including, but not limited to barns, corrals,
stock ponds, spring boxes, trails, road maintenance,
bunk and ranch houses, etc.

388.

See most politicians and non-profits for what they are.

Like gravity, there are powerful forces at work. County, state and federal governments, as well as many non-profits (which, by design, are immortal, tax-favored and devoid of the checks and balances of shareholders or voters) need to be held accountable; these entities will often do as little as possible under the cover of supposed and dubious good intentions and self-serving bureaucratic bloat.

Never assume that others think the same as you do. Unfortunately, the world is full of kooks, many who have important-sounding degrees from major universities, who will do everything they can to diminish property rights and other freedoms and pervert genuine stewardship, private ownership and industry.

To some, stewardship means turning a blind eye to monumental fire hazards; they ultimately seek to leave land fallow forever, absent of cowboys, farmers, miners, writers, hikers, hunters, fishermen, artists, as well as all of their pets and livestock, and farm and ranch infrastructure or its reasonable expansion; food, jobs, housing and the arts aren't priorities for them; their utopia is saving "open space" for an exclusive set of cronies and your name is not on their guest list.

Let's call a spade a spade. These zealots cherish their pale and vacuous ideals over your ruddy and raucous humanity. They undermine the legacy of the West in quiet conspiracy; over cups of herbal tea, they plot smugly behind the cherry-stained doors of their foundation board rooms and in closed-session government meetings.

In the holy name of "open space," while you are hard at work at your job or spending precious moments with your loved ones, they stack public meetings with those who, with unwavering and unequivocal fanaticism, advocate for more land-use restrictions, higher taxes and increased regulations.

I've seen this madness up close and wish that I was making it up; I am sounding the alarm and am asking you to resurrect and hold dear what is true, good and Constitutional. This isn't an advocacy for an insurrection, or for you to join the wild-eyed, unwashed or bigoted, but rather a clarion call for re-centering by any legal means necessary.

389.

Holding politicians by the proverbial short-hairs
doesn't make you a nut.
It means that you're aware.

Ask these simple questions:

*Why is it that nearly every item in our home, office and
on our highways are no longer made in the States?*

What are you doing about it?

390.

In the Sierra, when taking a break on a cattle drive, cowboys would light a campfire in the middle of the trail and keep a pot of coffee going; cowboys would ride around the perimeter of the herd to keep from losing strays; they also used bellwethers on cows in an effort to keep tabs.

(Courtesy of Dex Reeder.)

391.

It takes about as much lead to kill a wild boar as it does to kill a duck.

392.

What to look for when spotting an illegal pot farm: black irrigation drip pipes; zig-zag trails down a hill rather than ones which look more vertical; garbage in the middle of nowhere; an old trail that's been trimmed; chicken wire to keep out gophers; rock piles with Coke cans as trail markers; hand and boot prints on Power River gates (good for poachers, too); evidence of springs being tampered with; camo and blue tarps for check dams.

392.

Try to stay on the uphill side of a tree limb
that you're cutting with a chainsaw; try not to
cut above your head with a chainsaw; block the limb
when you can so that you don't hit the ground with
your saw.

(Courtesy of Jim Oneal.)

393.

Keep you chainsaw sharp and your 30-30 well-sighted.

(Courtesy of Jim Oneal.)

394.

Kick the wood pile before you pull a log in case there's
a rattler.
Make sure that you're wearing boots.

(Courtesy of Jim Oneal.)

395.

If a city slicker ever glasses people with
his rifle scope, don't let him ever hunt
on your property again.

(Courtesy of Jim Oneal.)

396.

A 400 hp Jeep can be fun to drive, but may scare away the game.

(Courtesy of Jeff Oneal, Jim's cousin.)

397.

Carry your rifle on the opposite side of the hill that you're climbing in case you trip and fall.

(Courtesy of Jim Oneal.)

398.

If you find out that a trespassing peak-bagger
is posting GPS coordinates and pictures of your
property, sick your attorney on him immediately.

(Based on a true story.)

399.

My sister is smarter than I am; I would work all summer loading hay in the barns and building fences; she
would raise and sell one steer at the County Fair and
make more money than I did.

The lesson here is that owners
can make more than laborers.

Author's youngest daughter riding
Copenhagen at the Wyoming ranch.

(Photograph from author's collection. August, 2015.)

400.

Bull Durham for everyday; tailor-mades for Christmas.

("Bull Durham" meant hand-rolled cigarettes.
"Tailor-mades" were bought cigarettes.)

(Courtesy of Jim Harvey.)

401.

Chances are that if you take the trail less traveled,
it won't lead you to water, livestock or game.

There are reasons that animals take a particular
trail over and over, despite what a
poet laureate may tell you.

A trail less traveled will lead you to
unpassable brush, a steep ravine,
a dried-up stock pond or a barbed-wire line
fence without a gate.

402.

Don't make a pet of your horse.

403.

I've seen people try to make pets of wild critters, some with more success than others. Baby raccoons are cute but when they get bigger, they'll rip apart the wires on your entertainment console.

404.

An unattended Aussie will get to your parakeet sooner
or later.

405.

Drive with your truck lights on during the day.
They're not that expensive to replace and it helps
people notice you on the road.

406.

If you're coming to a full stop on a highway,
expressway or mountain road, put on your emergency
blinkers and tap your brakes or risk getting rear-ended.

407.

Though it's a pain, keep accounting protocols.
I know three very successful business owners
who had big surprises involving their bookkeepers.

408.

If you're feeling anger towards someone,
including yourself, pray for him.

409.

If some things are weighing heavily
on your heart, write each one down
on a small slip of paper and place
it into a small wooden cigar box.

Call this box your "God box" and
let God worrying about the issue for awhile.
Revisit the box in a subsequent season
and many of the troubles may have
subsidied or disappeared.

410.

Getting to cash-flow positive is like hearing angels sing.

411.

A person putting down their spouse or family member only makes themselves look bad.

412.

If you really want to warm a cowgirl's heart,
do the dishes.

If she's made you dinner and asks you
if you liked it, tell her with a
straight face,

"Yes, because it was made with my
favorite ingredient... Your love."

413.

My grandfather, Hank, used to call my grandmother,
Pat, "B.G." This stood for "Beautiful Goodness."

My dad, "Bosco," called my mom, "Winnie,"
by the names of "Love Bucket" and "Sugar Pie."

My wife's nickname is "Gorgeous One."

If you're referring to your wife as "my old lady,"
change it up and write her a love letter.

414.

You'll learn more at a ranch cookhouse table
than at a four-year university.

But, if you can, attend college anyway.

415.

Never judge a farmer by his clothes or his car.

(He may be far wealthier than the doctor who's
driving the expensive foreign sports car
and living in a big house.)

416.

Never ride a colt while shipping calves.
Especially while helping the neighbors.

(Courtesy of Frank Maestri III.)

417.

Never trust your parking brake in rough country.

(Courtesy of Frank Maestri III.)

418.

Unshod horses do better in the mud.

(Courtesy of Frank Maestri III.)

419.

If it's a big and rough pasture you will never get them
all in one gather.
Especially while gathering yearlings.

(Courtesy of Frank Maestri III.)

420.

Let your calves drink before they cross the scale...
"A pint's a pound the world round!"

(Courtesy of Frank Maestri III.)

421.

Add a little peanut butter in with your refried beans and a little chicken broth in with your Spanish rice.

422.

If you're getting ready to brand or ship, plan well.

(An abridgement of the 7 Ps provided by Frank Maestri III.)

423.

Take an afternoon or two to lay out a map of your ranch and write down the names of the graves, old homesteads, fields, hills, trails, firebreaks, pastures, pond, springs and roads so that this history isn't lost when you pass away.

Photograph of Winnifred Coe Verbica
("Coe Kid" second from left).

(Photograph from HWC [Jr.] State Park archives, courtesy of Teddy Goodrich.)

424.

Older cowhands will encourage teenage boys to wrestle or box for the entertainment value. Having boxing gloves handy will cut down on the broken noses.

425.

The cowboy phrase "like shit through a green horn" referred to first-time cowhands on cattle drives who hadn't adjusted to the food.

(Courtesy of Jim Harvey.)

426.

Don't pull back too fast on your reins when you're
heeling, even if you're competing for time.

(Rodeos aren't for sissies. Doc Bert Johnson had to
report to President Ronald Reagan that his Secretary
of Commerce, Malcolm "Mac" Baldrige, passed away.
During a rodeo at Jack Roddy's ranch, the Secretary's
horse fell back onto him while he was heeling a calf;
the saddle horn drove into the roper's stomach, ruptur-
ing his aorta. Despite being airlifted to the hospital by
helicopter, Mr. Baldrige didn't make it.)

427.

Angus may not fare well in brutally hot, high desert cli-
mates. Brahman or Brangus have better odds of surviv-
ing, but the Brahma can be difficult to round up.

(Courtesy of Dex Reeder and Doc Bert Johnson.)

428.

Keep your sense of humor.

(In the *Los Rancheros Visitadores* ride in 1990, Doc Bert Johnson won the race between a group of mules; at the finish line, Doc Bert yelled up at President Reagan and asked if he would get in a picture with the Democrat mascot. When Reagan came down for the picture, he asked Doc Bert if, since the mule won, could they both agree that it must be a Republican mule.)

429.

If you're poor and do odd things,
you'll be labeled crazy. If you're
wealthy, you'll be admired as eccentric.

(One nouveaux ranch owner knows little about riding
and even less about cattle. He decided to buy
a string of Argentinian Polo ponies because he
fantasizes about playing polo. This will just make
an old cowhand shake his head.)

430.

If you ain't the lead horse, you'll never get a change of scenery.

(Courtesy of Jack Roddy.)

431.

Live one day as a lion rather than your whole life as a mouse.

(Courtesy of Jack Roddy.)

432.

All you get sitting on a fence is a sore ass.

(Courtesy of Jack Roddy.)

433.

A book is never finished,
only abandoned.

*(Robin Chapman paraphrasing an aphorism
attributed to DaVinci about art.)*

Each of us sense this as kindred spirits,
I imagine:

The engraver finishes up scroll work
on a single-action Army revolver;

The Mexican craftsman stamps the final tooling on
a saddle or belt;

The Western painter touches up dust clouds
under horses' hooves;

The modern cowboy lifts up a pen
from the last stanza of a poem,

just before he puts on his hat
and heads out a warped screen door

to feed his cattle.

434.

If someone's a U.S. Veteran, service member,
or your father-in-law,
serve them your aged Scotch or better wine.

You can pour the green stuff for
politicians, foundation lawyers, and
bureaucrats."

435.

Real cowboys don't tailgate.

Relax. There's plenty of time left.

436.

If someone cuts you off, try flashing a
peace sign rather than your middle finger.

(As my dad used to advise me,
"Rise above it.")

437.

Prescription pain killers and sleeping meds
used improperly can take the toughest cowboys out.

438.

Don't throw out last year's fishing and hunting licenses
until you receive the new ones; you may need
them as proof when you're wrangling with a
bureaucrat.

439.

If you have food on your table,
shake hands with a farmer and
thank her.

440.

A cowboy's legacy is best kept alive outside of
museums.

441.

Make peace with your family's history.

A peek at the childhood photos of
your forefathers will fill you with
compassion rather than resentment.

442.

God has many names and manifestations,
including "the Great Outdoors."

443.

Stop asking,
"Why does God let bad things happen
to good people?"

Start asking "how" instead and
see what you can do to make a difference.

444.

Have some tarps handy. It'll keep you from
having to beg neighbors when the big rain comes.

(Courtesy of Paul Mulholand.)

Author's wife, Tiffany Verbica, overlooking a field of lupen wildflowers at the brick house at *Rancho San Felipe*.

An elite athlete and trail runner,
Tiffany was the top female finisher at the
Henry Coe 5k/10k Fun Run and Walk
in 2014 and 2015. The race is an "out-and-back"
at Hunting Hollow on the fire break road.

(Photograph from the author's collection.)

445.

"Even foreign waters look familiar when the fish are biting."

(Angelo Canepa as quoted by his son, Jeff Canepa)

446.

Near Silver City, New Mexico, to cook a rattlesnake for dinner, a cowboy would kill a snake, lay it on a Yucca plant and light the plant on fire.

(Courtesy of John Savage.)

447.

Tell your wife that she's pretty,
your children that you're proud of them
and your parents that you're grateful -- often.

448.

Tongue-in-cheek javelina recipe:

Dig a 4' x 4' 4' ditch. Fill ditch with brush. Burn the brush and then layer with rocks. Then layer with brush and branches. Burn and then get a gunny sack. Place the javelina in the gunny sack, drop into ditch. Cover gunny sack liberally with beer. Place pine boughs on top of the gunny sack and cover it thoroughly with sand. Walk away, come back in 24 hours and hope like hell you never find the javelina.

(Recipe courtesy of Jim Harvey.)

449

There are lots of ways to skin a cat, but the easiest way
is to let someone else do it.

(Courtesy of Bob Hoffmann, a lumberman.)

450

A drunk friend who wants to drive isn't your friend
until he's sober. If he won't let you drive, find another,
safer way to get home.

451

A machine gun will climb on you in a split second, so hold on to it firmly.

(Courtesy of a rancher who prefers to remain anonymous.)

452

When you're shooting ducks in the cold, don't wear gloves which are slippery. You could have a loaded gun jump out of your hands when you pull up on birds. Wear gloves which have a non-slip surface instead.

(Courtesy of Don Huntley.)

453

Don't let your fly drag – either on top of the water or below it. Insects don't drag.

(Courtesy of David Sage, Avid Fly Fisherman, Grand Lakes Stream, Maine)

454

Advice on fly fishing? Keep at it. You'll get better.

(Courtesy of David Sage, Avid Fly Fisherman, Grand
Lakes Stream, Maine)

455

Whiskey's for drinking. Water's for fighting.

(Courtesy of Marty Kropelnicki, a water utility executive, citing a Western maxim often misattributed to Mark Twain)

456

Spending weakens a family. Investing strengthens a family.

(Courtesy of Barry Swenson, Isabel Valley Ranch)

457.

You can't make chicken feed out of chicken manure.

(Translated: you need the right materials to do the right job.)

(Mark Garrison of the Garrison Ranch quoting his dad, Charles.)

458.

Don't let your kids cut cots. It's done with speed using a wicked, hooked knife and requires a deft touch. Haste combined with inexperience can lead to the loss of a finger.

(Courtesy of Rob Christopher of the Christopher Ranch, Gilroy, Calif.)

459.

Picking French prunes is easier on the young.

Once the prunes are shaken from the trees, you're on your knees all day loading buckets. The wiser kids wear knee pads.

(Courtesy of Rob Christopher of the Christopher Ranch, Gilroy, Calif.)

460.

Measure twice. Cut once.

(Barry Swenson of the Isabel Valley Ranch quoting a
proverb often used by his grandfather.)

I grew up
2012

I grew up with cattlemen
in the middle of a valley

at the end of a dead-end road:

They're long gone,
but I can still see them

through the dust,
casting their
dirt-and-diesel shadows

over the abandoned barns,
blacksmith shops,
and ramshackle ranch houses,

past the Eucalyptus trees,
oaks and sycamores

past the wood shakes
and weeping willows.

I earned my spurs with them,

dipped into the same
cans of Copenhagen.
I field-dressed wild boar
and dried brine-soaked strips
of beef in jerky houses with them.

And, I will salute them.

They're still

branding and ear-marking bawling calves.

They're still heading and heeling
steers in the hills to
treat them for pinkeye.

They're still mending barbed-wire fences,

and filling D-9 Cats with fuel:

on hallowed ground in my mind.

They're still swearing and
wearing their sweat-stained brims.

They're still spitting into the
palms of their hands

to put out their cigarettes.
(I can hear the sizzle:

it's like a cherry
held in the teeth
of my ear.)

They talk of tits and ass,
of boots and trucks and heifers,

of Labradors, Queensland heelers
and 30-30's.

This was years before

taxes broke the owners
like stubborn Mustangs,

before the city folk
came in like rustlers,
and bought up all the land,

before they ripped up this history
under a plow of mediocrity,

turning over clods in the dry ground,
for a crop of star thistle,

before the name of each ranch
was perverted to "open space"

and dedicated in
back-patting ceremonies
to termites, tar weed and
doe-eyed docents.

I grew up here:

where you learned
to roll out of a rabbit-punch,

and to shut up when you were told.

You learned to laugh
at the same drunken jokes,

but not to laugh too hard,

or the crazy-eyed joker
would turn on you,

fast and subtle,
like a rattler,

but without the warning:
and strike your jaw with

the back of a hand
which hit like a hammer.

I can hear them asking
for one last
hand of poker at
the bunkhouse dinner table.

I'll deal them in.

Every single last
one of them.

They're all in
for the final pot.

All of this happened,
in the pendulum
of summer after summer:

mowing through the months,
and leaving all of these memories
in a stream of rows

which looked as if they were
hand-painted upon the fields
with a pallet knife

chock-full of ochre:

Each story bound
in a bale,
wound with steel wire,

hauled onto a flatbed
in the heat,

and stacked into the loft
of one's mind,

to be fed off of later.

This is my library:

under walnut trees
which would canker

white-washed timbers
with black dots.

I grew up with these cowboys
who would admonish me
and say that

it's not safe

for a candy-assed boy:

you may never amount to much,
they would remind me,

and if you're not careful,
the world will be overrun

by doped-up hippies
and small-town hookers,

who will
screw you out of your
last dollar:

It's fluid in the lungs:
pneumonia in the middle
of a hot summer:

a jug of warm Sangria wine
nested in a tin-tub of
rolled oat-grain and molasses.

God save you from
the roughshod
of our ramblings,
they would confide,

they're worse
than being struck down
by lightening
in the middle
of a hayfield,

or getting kicked
square in the forehead
while shoeing a horse.

If years later,

you hear our musings scraping
under the braided rugs
in the ranch house of these lost decades,

take a shotgun to the floorboards
until you can get the little
bastards to stop.

Turn up the volume of the radio
in this tenement house in homage,
tune it to a Western song:

here, in the middle of nowhere, and
then walk past this plywood door.
Leave behind the rusted hay hooks
and cement sinks

and never come back.

How could they know how right they'd be?

How hard they would probably laugh
to know that the skinny kid
would be the last one to defend them,

and not let time cut off the testicles
of their memory:

to polish the German silver buckles
and Hamley saddles,
to remember their names
in black and white photos,

to stand up their statues,
in the real cowboy hall of fame.

*P*eter Coe Verbica grew up on *Rancho San Felipe*, a commercial cattle ranch in Northern California. He earned his BA in English from Santa Clara University, a JD from Santa Clara University School of Law, and an MS from the Massachusetts Institute of Technology. He is married, has four daughters and works in the wealth management group of an investment bank.

Acknowledgements

This little book of *Hard-Won Cowboy Wisdom (Not Necessarily in Order of Importance.)* is dedicated to

my dad, **Bosco,** who was in the Pacific in WWII in the Army Air Corps., All-American in baseball at U of A, a wrangler at Estes Park, a coach who took his high school teams to the state championships and was uniformly generous to all;

my grandfather, **Hank,** who was a two-miler at Stanford, held the record for over a decade, smoked a box of Teamo Maduro cigars a day, and presided over Rancho San Felipe with an iron fist;

great grandfather, **Harry**, who sat straight
on a horse, dressed impeccably, had jaw-
dropping penmanship, was an amazing
marksman and homesteaded the heart of
Coe State Park with his brother, **Charles**;

great, great grandfather, **Henry**, an early settler
in California, who owned "the Willows" and
"the Phoenix" gold mine in Amador County;

as well as all of the cowboys I've known
over the years, including **Lawrence
"Phil" Phillips**, a reluctant fiddler
who could fix just about anything;

Bill McNeil, who always treated me
like a grandson and taught me how
to build a decent fence and gate;

Charlie Maggini, world's champion roper,
Cowboy Hall of Fame awardee, and horse
trainer extraordinaire who helped me
appreciate a well-trained cutting horse;

Dane Sorenson, a true, country
gentleman with an infectious laugh;

Jake Nunez, who once reportedly wooed
a maid by putting a bed and its frame
in the middle of a field of wild oats;

Clifford "Barry" Swenson, co-owner of the
Isabel Valley Ranch and Alturas Ranches with
a nose for value and the patience of Job;

Elmer "Reese" Reese, who was an amazing
shot and did the work of ten men;

George Becker, even though
he was a Democrat;

Salvador Prado, who stood patiently
with his wife, **Virginia**, while my aunt,
Nancy, painted their portrait;

Don Kidder, who taught me hunter safety
as a boy and coached my grandmother,
Pat, into becoming a crack shot;

Verle Lybbert, who shod horses for
most of the ranches near where I grew up
and his world-champion son, **Chris**;

Chuck Kessinger, the world's
hardest-working veterinarian;

Jim Harvey, from the Sundog Ranch,
who told me what it was like to grow up
without running water or electricity and
how to make a horse-hair cinch by hand;

Ben Parker, the only cowboy that I know of
who had a stuffed tiger's head in his living room;

ranch manager, **Ray Parker**, who says
in five words what it takes me fifty;

Bob McLaughlin, who led by example
and helped me get up off of the mat;

Bennie Nunes, who saved my mom from a
mountain lion at Pine Ridge one summer;

Duane Hagen, who guided my
dad and me through the mountains
above Cody in search of elk;

John "Johnny Mac" McNicholas
and **Bob Hoffman**, who enjoy
writing Country Western songs;

Bob Beck, who renewed my interest
in the farm and ranch lifestyle with
his unbridled enthusiasm;

Dex Reeder, who's never forgotten his roots or
priorities and is a keeper of the Cowboy Code;

Jim Oneal, co-owner of the Isabel
Ranch who keeps the traditions of his
dad and granddad alive and well,

Carolyn Straub, **Teddy Goodrich** and
Coe Park Ranger **Barry Breckling** (ret.),
historians who help preserve Sada Coe
Robinson, HWC [Jr.] California State
Park and the Coe family's legacy;

Frank Maestri III, who's ranched in
California, Nevada, Texas, and Wyoming,
as well as been a cowboy and buckaroo in
Arizona, Arkansas, Idaho, Louisiana, Oregon,
Oklahoma, Montana, New Mexico, and Utah,

the **Santos**, **Reese**, **Kidder** and
Richmond families who always made
me feel welcome in their homes,

"Doc" Bert Johnson. the *"Roping Doc,"* master story-teller,

Jack Roddy, team roper and World's Champion steer-wrestler who still remembers many of the cattlemen I grew up with on the Coe Ranch;

Paul Mulholand, who taught me how to quickly set up and anchor a canvas tent and what real friendship is;

the **DiNapoli, Lopes, Fox, Schumb, Marani, DeMar, James, Brandenberg, McDonald, Moore, Jennsen, Morgan, Wood, Collins, Smythe**, and **Cannino** families, each exemplary in their own unique way;

Jeff Rickert, Tim Bowman, John Flolo, George Collins, and **Ron Fritzke**, and other friends loyal to my dad;

Louis Nisich, former boxer and body guard who did major grading to connect parts of the Coe Ranch ("the Second Bench") using dynamite and earth movers;

Robin Chapman, author, historian and television personality who turns good research into an even better story;

David Packard, tech entrepreneur and former U.S. Deputy Secretary of Defense, who helped me in quiet ways and never needed any credit;

President Ronald Reagan, literate, considerate, witty, steadfast, and supported by Republican families such as mine over the years;

President George W. Bush, who complimented my dad's Tony Lama's and, as a fellow Christian, called him "brother;"

Hon. Joe Foss, WWII ace, Governor, Commissioner, public-speaker and long-time, close hunting friend of my dad, "Bosco;"

M. Sam Araki, former head of Lockheed Martin Missiles and Space, who's never forgotten his farming roots, pursues subject matter expertise with a vengeance, and taught me how to work harder than I thought possible;

the many supporters of STV and STI
whose efforts ultimately helped us make
the world a slightly safer place;

Ralph Cowden, avid fisherman and the
remarkable force behind SPARC;

Dan McCranie, who helps preserve
the legacy of the West and agrees that
tearing out stock ponds under the guise
of conservation is plain wrong-headed;

friends at the **Family Club** (including Tim
Morgan), **SOKOSJ** (including **Don Witt,
Finn Jenssen** and **Brian Rauschhuber),
Rotary Club of San Jose, SVSAR, St. Claire
Club, Society of California Pioneers**, the
**Santa Clara County Society of Pioneers,
SPARC, Santa Clara University (including
Ron Hansen, Diane Dreher, John Firth,
Steve Privett, SJ, Wm. Rewak, SJ, Juan
Velasco,** and **Michael Malone), Society of
Jesus, Pine Ridge Association, Catamaran
Literary Magazine** (including **Catherine
Segurson** and **Zack Rogow), TLC** in Aptos,
SJSU (including **Lydia Ortega** and **Avantika
Rohatgi), FXR** (including **Ross Flaven**) and
Mt. Moriah who encourage my creativity;

friends **George McCown**, **Jean McCown**, **Marianne "Poppy" Tanner**, who used to ride with Winnie Coe Verbica at the Coe Ranch, **Jack and Lurlene Bickel**, **Evie Richmond**, **Bill McCollam**, **Jack and Lurlene Bickel**, **Lillian Surkova**, **Bart Berardo,** and **Steve Blach**;

cousins, including, but not limited to, **Mae Lim Harrison**, **Norma and Tom Coe**, **Tom M. Coe**, **Irene Robinson Lim**, **Bonnie Robinson Nazarenko**, **Don Verbica**, who put up with my curiosity;

my sister, **Pearle**, who lives on a farm and spent years gathering cattle and caring for horses on Rancho San Felipe as well;

my wife, **Tiffany**, four daughters, **Vanessa**, **Madeline**, **Caroline** and **Elizabeth**, in-laws, **Nick** and **Lenny**, and family, who "have my back;"

and many others who should be included, but for my waning memory, who share an affection for the American West and cowboy culture.

HWC, Jr. proud of his cow horse.

(Photograph from the author's collection.)

Made in the USA
San Bernardino, CA
10 January 2016